# Table of Contents

Go to PodcastLaunchAudio.com for a FREE audio download of "Podcast Launch".

# 4 Free Podcasting Resources for you!

1) **FreePodcastCourse.com:** This is a free 15-day Podcasting course that brings to life everything we will be talking about in this book. Every day for 15 days you'll receive a video tutorial that will take you one step further along your Podcasting journey. This is a step one to step done Podcasting course, and these tutorials will ensure that YOU are prepared to IGNITE!

   >> Click or tap here << to join the Free Podcast Course today! (Link: FreePodcastCourse.com)

2) **Free Podcast Course Podcast:** This is a 20-episode Podcast that will take you through every step of the Podcasting process, from creating, to growing, to monetizing a Podcast. We'll also be dissecting key topics such as *The four biggest mistake Podcasters make.'* and *'The three most important things every Podcaster must know.'*

   >> Click or tap here << to subscribe in iTunes (Link: EOFire.com/fpc1414)

   >> Click or tap here << to subscribe in Stitcher (Link: EOFire.com/fpc1515)

3) **LIVE Podcast Workshop!** Join John Lee Dumas every Wednesday as he hosts a FREE and LIVE Podcast Workshop. This workshop will be jammed packed with Podcasting knowledge for Podcasters at every stage in their journey; the beginner, intermediate, and the expert.

   >> Click or tap here << to claim your spot at the next LIVE Podcast Workshop! (link: PodcastersParadise.com)

4) **A streaming Podcast Workshop TODAY!** That's right, 7-days a week you can join John Lee Dumas on a FREE streaming Podcast Workshop where he will share how to Create ~ Grow ~ & Monetize a Podcast, as well as 2 super hacks that 99% of Podcasters are not doing that you need to be!

   >> Click here << to join a streaming Podcast Workshop TODAY! (Link: EOfire.com/streamingPW)

# Note from the Author

Hi fellow and future Podcasters! John Lee Dumas here, founder and host of EntrepreneurOnFire, a business Podcast where I interview today's most inspiring and successful Entrepreneurs 7-days a week. EntrepreneurOnFire was awarded 'Best of iTunes 2013' and has amassed over 13 million downloads since launch in September of 2012. Podcasting has been such an amazing journey and I am excited you are considering taking your leap into this fascinating world (or furthering your current knowledge).

The number one question I faced when I launched was *"How on earth are you going to monetize a Podcast John?"* Well, I did not have the answers then, but I have plenty of them now. Every month, we publish our income reports to share with you what is working in the Podcasting world, and what is not. Feel free to peruse our income reports at EntrepreneurOnFire.com/income

**Podcast Launch** will provide you with a complete guide to launching your own Podcast. If this book **FIRES** you up as much as I think it will, we will be excitedly awaiting you in Podcasters' Paradise, the #1 Podcasting community in the world.

We do a free and live webinar **every week** and we hope you join us! Sign up for our next one at PodcastersParadise.com.

For more details about Podcasters' Paradise...read below:

## Podcasters' Paradise is made up of 3 components:

1. **Over 200 Video Tutorials:** Podcasters' Paradise has step-by-step video tutorials for Podcasters at **every** level.

   **Beginners:** Step-by-step video tutorials on how to **Create & Launch** your Podcast.

   **Intermediates:** Video tutorials on how to **Grow** your Podcast audience.

   **Experts:** Video tutorials on how to **Monetize** your Podcast!

2. **A Thriving Community:** Nothing is more important than building relationships with other Podcasters, and the Podcasters' Paradise private Facebook group is the #1 Podcasting community in the world! Exchange honest reviews, find guests for your show, find shows to be a guest on, practice your interview skills, and receive feedback, advice, tips, tools, and tactics galore!

   We also will match you up with an accountability partner who is at a similar place in their journey, which will give you a partner in crime right from the start!

3. **Monthly Webinars With Today's Top Podcasters:** Join us as we invite host exclusive webinars with top Podcasters. Past guests are Amy Porterfield, Pat Flynn, Lewis Howes, Michael Hyatt, James Altucher, Ramit Sethi, Chris Ducker

and more! These webinars are live so you can ask questions, but if you miss the webby for any reason, we record and post every one in the Podcasters' Paradise membership site so you can watch (or re-watch) at your leisure.

**Monthly Q&A Sessions with John Lee Dumas:** Every month I host a hangout where you can join me live and ask any question you have in regards to Podcasting. I answer every question over the course of the hour+ hangout, and we have a blast!

If all this has you fired up for Podcasters' Paradise, you can lock in the lowest price we will ever offer from this day forward AND lifetime membership.

Simply >> click here << fill out the order form, and welcome to Paradise!

*\*\*We are always increasing the cost of Podcasters' Paradise as we add value, and we are always adding value, so the price you can lock in today is the lowest price we will ever offer, but will be raised in the near future.*

*\*\*We have a 100% satisfaction guarantee, so if Podcasters' Paradise is not for you, we will happily refund you your full payment, and wish you the best on your journey!*

# Preface

So, you're thinking about starting a podcast? GOOD IDEA! Seriously though, Podcasting is exploding for a number of reasons, which I'm about to unveil in this Preface.

Remember, the purchase of *Podcast Launch* gives you access to multiple video tutorials I've created just for you. You will be able to access each and every one with your purchase. I am truly excited for you to begin your journey, so let's dive right in. Prepare to ignite!

PodcastLaunchVideos.com

## The Podcasting Explosion

There are many reasons why Podcasting is experiencing such incredible growth. Below are ten reasons I find most compelling:

### 1. Offers on demand, passionate, and targeted content

Think about this following phrase. *With Podcasts, you don't have to say NO to something to say YES to Podcasts.* What does that mean exactly? Well, Podcasts can be consumed while driving, running, folding laundry, walking your dog, exercising, and any number of similar activities that require some semblance of focus. You don't have to say NO to any of the above activities to say YES to Podcasting, and that is why so many people are so willing to give 30+ minutes of their time to listen to your show, as they are able to be productive in other activities simultaneously!

I remember my commute to work back in the day. I was starting to wonder how many times I could listen to Miley Cyrus before seeking professional help. How often have we asked ourselves, *"Do radio stations conspire to all have commercials on at the SAME time?"* What if we could walk out the door in the morning excited about our commute to work?

With podcasts, we can be.

Let's use a random example to illustrate my point:

Sally is 42 years old, lives in upstate New York, and commutes 45 minutes to work at a greenhouse where she happily spends the next eight hours of her day doing something she loves: gardening.

Sally also has three kids – all teenagers – and they're quite demanding, to say the least. Her free time at home is a percentage point below zero, and sometimes that bothers her.

You see, Sally loves all things plant-related, and if it were up to her, she'd be studying and learning about gardens with every spare moment she has. But while she's at work, she is dealing with customers and administrative duties all day, and that leaves her NO time to improve upon her craft.

She knows there are so many things she could be educating herself about if only she had the time. But as soon as Sally's head hits her pillow at night, she has about two minutes before it's "goodnight Sally!" Before she knows it, Sally has been on the same "Better Homes and Gardens" page for three weeks.

Sally also slightly resents her 45-minute drive to work each day. It's long, boring, and she gets nothing accomplished.

Over a coffee break one day at work, her co-worker, Vanessa, mentions that she has been listening to a podcast called *Griselda the Green Thumb*. "What's a podcast?" Sally asks in honest bewilderment. Five minutes later, Sally can't wait to get home and load her iPod full of this free, targeted content about a subject she so loves.

The next morning, Sally jumps in her car, and before she even turns on her seat heater she has episode #1 pumping through her eight car speakers. 45 joyful minutes later, Sally is letting her car idle in the parking lot so she can scribble down some notes about petunias and daisies.

Sally has discovered the wonderful world of Podcasting, and her car rides, walks, and workout sessions will never be the same.

## 2. It's free

When you listen to podcasts, you're hearing from experts who are dispensing advice and sharing insights in what feels like a one-on-one session. Were this truly the case, it would cost you thousands of dollars every time you listened to one.

Podcast hosts and interviewees can afford (literally and figuratively) to give this incredible advice away for free because they are reaching hundreds – if not thousands – of eager ears, allowing them to become authority figures to a huge audience who is growing to know, like and trust them.

As the content continues to be dispensed, the audience continues to grow because they are getting great, actionable, highly valued content for free. A veritable win-win!

### 3. Accessible from Smartphones

Do you know anyone these days who is active in the online world but who doesn't have a Smartphone? Even Blackberry made sure to include a podcast app on their latest device.

Smartphones, WiFi, 4G networks, iTunes, Soundcloud, and Stitcher Radio have allowed people around the world to consume streaming, online content with the swipe of a finger. With this computer in my pocket, downloading and/or streaming podcasts has never been easier, and my little white ear buds have never been so tangled.

### 4. Readily available on tablets

Ok, when my 88-year-old grandmother told me her most favorite possession in the world was her iPad, I realized that we have now entered a new era.

We are seldom out of reach from a screen that allows us to connect in an instant. Thanks to Facetime, I see my cousin's face WAY more than I see my next-door neighbor's face, despite my neighbor living 12 feet away and my cousin 3,000 miles.

Also, I am always just one swipe away from seeing if any of my favorite podcasts have released a new episode, and it's like Christmas morning when they have.

## 5. At your fingertips, thanks to Wi-Fi

We live in a world that does not tether us to a cord and a square shaped hole in a wall. We live in a world where we can connect to some crazy airwaves that allow us to zip around to any place our heart desires on the World Wide Web. Whether we are 30,000 feet in the air or within a baseballs throw of an Internet café in Zanzibar, once we are connected, hello dolly!

## 6. Provides the opportunity for an intimate connection

Words on a page are black, white and cold. Podcasts allow for a connection that is nothing short of intimate. We are human beings, and we **connect** with **voices**. I cannot tell you how many people have emailed me with variations of the phrase, *"John, I listen to your podcast every day and although we haven't met, I feel as though we are close* *friends.*"

Do you think bloggers get that kind of email often? Nope. Audio connects us in a way the written word never could, and Podcasting is an amazing example of this truth. As a podcaster, you are literally inside the ears of your listeners. The kind of trust and intimacy that is built over time with this type of medium creates a very strong bond. As a trusted adviser and friend, be sure you honor that bond with genuine recommendations, suggestions, and direction.

**7. Gives you instant authority and credibility**

Let's be honest: I'm nowhere near the ranks of Barbara Corcoran, Seth Godin, Gary Vaynerchuk, Tim Ferriss, or many other successful Entrepreneurs I have had the distinct honor of speaking with one-on-one on EntrepreneurOnFire. However, like most things in life, we are 'guilty' by association.

My status is automatically elevated because of the quality of my guests. The fact that they deem it worthwhile to bestow upon me, a mere mortal, several minutes of their precious time speaks volumes to my audience, whom I dearly refer to as *Fire Nation*.

Barbara Corcoran is a great example of this. Back on December 28th, 2012, Barbara spent 45 minutes of her time on EntrepreneurOnFire. She did so with the realization her message would be heard by thousands of listeners for years to come. If I had just asked Barbara to chat one-on-one with me for 45 minutes, I am sure I would have received a kind but curt, *"No, but thank you."* from her assistant.

When you work hard and create a show that has a large and engaged audience, you too will have access to the experts in your industry who simply don't have the time to share their expertise and knowledge with people on a one-one basis.

## 8. Affords you a broad reach

14 days after I launched EntrepreneurOnFire, I decided to take a look at my demographics. Much to my surprise, EntrepreneurOnFire had already been downloaded and subscribed to in over 100 countries around the world. 100! EntrepreneurOnFire is now downloaded daily in over 145 countries including EVERY country in South America, 90% of Africa, all of Europe, and many other parts of the globe.

Some of my favorite emails are from people who are admitting to using Google Translate before emailing me, as their audible understanding of English is much better than their written word.

It is incredible to picture young Entrepreneurs in rural towns – in 3rd world countries – downloading EntrepreneurOnFire at the one local Internet café, and then staying up late at night listening to episodes over and over.

I hear first-hand every day how EntrepreneurOnFire is helping people all over the world dream dreams that would have otherwise never existed. The potential reach you have with a podcast is only limited to the four corners of the earth. Never before has one microphone wielded so much power. It's time to light up the airwaves Fire Nation!

**9. Delivers amazing statistics:**

You are only as good as you can prove you are, especially when it comes to podcasting. How can you prove you are worth the precious time it takes a busy Entrepreneur to come on your show and share their life story? How can you prove to yourself that you are reaching enough people to make your time expenditure worthwhile?

Well, my friends, this is yet another reason why podcasting is so powerful. Does anyone REALLY know how many people are listening to a certain radio station at any given time? Or actually watching a specific TV station? Not really. However, with podcasts, you can measure the exact number of downloads with extreme accuracy.

As you can imagine, this is very valuable information – actual numbers that we can use to base some pretty solid assumptions off of. Do I hold any illusions of grandeur that every one of my 950,000+ downloads a month is listened to in its entirety? Nope. But I do know that I can measure the growth of my audience and make some pretty solid estimates.

Stitcher Radio even measures the amount of time someone listens to your podcast, so you can study patterns and see how long is too long, or how short is too short. These statistics are very valuable, and I use them to promote EntrepreneurOnFire all the time.

Here is a snippet from an email I send out to potential interviewees: *"We would be thrilled to have you as a guest on our show, EntrepreneurOnFire, a top ranked Business, averaging over 950,000 unique downloads each month in over 145 countries. We understand you have a busy schedule, and that's why we've developed an efficient, 30-minute audio interview over Skype. We have an awesome lineup thus far, including Seth Godin, Gary Vaynerchuk, Barbara Corcoran, Guy Kawasaki, Chris Brogan, Eric Ries, and Tim Ferriss... just to name a few."*

Do you think most Entrepreneurs find 30 minutes in their schedule after reading that? Yep.

The same goes for potential sponsors and advertisers. Statistics provide measure and value, and podcasts have one of the most accurate measuring tools out there. For that, we should all be VERY grateful!

**10. The ability to monetize:**

As I mentioned in the Note From The Author section,

EntrepreneurOnFire has found many ways to monetize. We have multiple 5-figure monthly income streams, all of which add up to over $200,000 **every month**, which we share in detail here: EOFire.com/Income.

EntrepreneurOnFire generates over $60,000 every month from sponsorships alone, and I share some great insider information on Podcast Sponsorships in a detailed post I wrote here: EOFire.com/PodcastSponsorships

Affiliate income, mentoring, products, services and masterminds are just a few other ways we are able to monetize. Note that the amount of income we bring in through these different streams is only possible because of the size of our audience, and Podcasters' Paradise is the place where we offer all the tutorials on how you can create the same for your podcast.

# My Journey

In this section I will share my journey and bring you full circle on how EntrepreneurOnFire came to be. If this is of no interest to you, please skip ahead to Chapter 1 and dive right into the creation process of your podcast. No hard feelings...promise!

I grew up in a small town in Southern Maine, and at 18 I headed to Providence College in Rhode Island on a ROTC scholarship. After four years of embracing the college lifestyle and training hard as a cadet, I was commissioned as a 2nd Lieutenant in the US ARMY. The year was 2002, and we were the first Officers' commissioned post 9/11, meaning we all knew we had some serious business ahead of us.

After training in Washington, Kentucky and Kansas, I was off to the desert with the 1st Infantry Division as an Armor Platoon leader (Tanks) in charge of 16 men and equipment, to boot. We spent 13 months in Iraq, where we fought terrorists, built schools, water treatment facilities, and helped train the new Iraqi Army. 13 months later, our tour of duty was over, but let us never forget the hero's who gave the ultimate sacrifice while serving the USA.

I spent the rest of my active duty time at Fort Riley Kansas, and in 2006, I entered the reserves. At that moment in time, I was as free as I had ever been: 26 years old, plenty of savings, no responsibilities (minus myself), and looking for adventure.

Over the next three years, my journey consisted of a variety of things. I started off with a four-month stay in Guatemala, living with a family and taking in the culture. Then, I spent a semester in Law School, where I learned a lot, but mostly that Law was not the path for me. After that, I took a job in finance with John Hancock in Boston, and I spent a great 18 months living in a city I loved with great friends and a job that was exciting – for a time.

Next, it was off to the Big Apple to give it a go with a tech start-up. I loved living in NYC, but the job itself never materialized into what I was hoping for, and so I heeded the call from the Gold Coast. I took off for San Diego in 2009 with no job and no friends awaiting.

What was waiting for me was a 325 square foot studio located two blocks from the Pacific Ocean. Soon enough, I fell into a great Real Estate gig, and I found myself with a group of friends who knew how to take advantage of the warm weather and the relaxed environ.

After a wonderful 18-month stint in SoCal, I was offered a potential career opportunity that, at the age of 31, I was pretty excited to take. This opportunity was way across the country in my home state of Maine, a place I had left 13 years prior.

I was being offered a position at a Commercial Real Estate firm, one that came with a partnership track if I worked hard and was successful. I knew it was time to get serious about where my professional life was heading, and so I jumped at the opportunity. In June of 2011, I joined The Dunham Group based out of Portland, Maine.

I spent the next year hard at work, immersing myself in all the differences I found between Residential Real Estate in San Diego and Commercial Real Estate in Maine. I truly learned a lot, and I believe if I had been born 20 years earlier, I would have found a great career in Commercial Real Estate.

However, we live in very exciting times, and by June of 2012 I realized there was too much out there I wanted to explore to stay in my current role. Fortified by Chris Guillenbeau's "The $100 Startup" and a trip to Blogworld in NYC, I was ready to make the break into the exciting – and terrifying – world of Entrepreneurism.

## The Birth Of EntrepreneurOnFire

Let me take you back to San Diego for a moment so I can share how my love affair with podcasting began. My job in Residential Real Estate required that I spend A LOT of time in the car. I was often times driving the length of San Diego County daily.

I soon grew incredibly tired of hearing the same old songs on the radio, and when I tried to make the switch to talk radio, the randomness of it all and the long commercials killed me. I had to find something else – quick – and it was not my scratched version of Jock Jams circa 1995.

One morning while I was bemoaning this annoyance to my neighbor and friend, Susan, she looked at me quizzically and asked, "Why don't you download some podcasts?" I looked at Susan, puzzled, and asked, "Say what?"

30 minutes later I was excitedly browsing through a brand new world of incredibly on demand, passionate and targeted content. Oh, and did I mention this stuff is free?

From that moment on I was a podcasting fool, and I would not leave my apartment without an iPod chock full of great podcasts. I started with the big boys: Mr. Dave Ramsey, Wall Street Journal, and APM Marketplace all filled my now-energized car rides. I was finally in control of the content playing through my car speakers, and I never missed a word with that blessed play/pause button.

As I continued to delve deeper into podcasts, I began to fall in love with the shows that held a little more personal flavor. Soon, Mixergy, The Rise To The Top, and Smart Passive Income were replacing the corporate and impersonal podcasts. Andrew Warner, David Siteman Garland, Pat Flynn and others soon became a voice I came to know, like and trust. They became pseudo friends, as their banter kept my drives interesting and lively.

The years went by, but my love for these podcasts never withered. I took this love with me on my cross-country move, and the familiar voices were now with me on the country roads of Maine. I began to crave the episodes where the hosts interviewed a successful and inspiring Entrepreneurs. I loved hearing their journeys, and I couldn't get enough.

I was consuming these types of episodes much faster than they were being produced. Most podcasts air once a week, and I was flying through years of content in mere months. I needed more, but it just wasn't out there.

It was on a drive late one night when I was still far away from my destination that my "AHA" moment happened. A light bulb bright enough to engulf the dark roadway popped from my head. One great podcast ended, and when I clicked next, there was nothing. I was out of podcasts. No mas, and I knew my favorite podcasters' schedules by heart. None were being published for days, and I had some serious miles ahead of me.

What was I going to do? Go back to the radio? No – I promised myself I would never fall back into Miley's warm embrace. It was then that I realized there MUST be others out there, others like me who drove alone or hit the gym daily. There must be others who want – no, NEED – fresh content on a DAILY basis.

This podcast I had dreamed up in my mind did not exist, and in a moment of clarity I knew I was going to be the one to create it. I was going to create a podcast that released a fresh episode every day. It was at that moment the spark was lit; it was at that moment EntrepreneurOnFire was born.

## Building The Platform

Finally, at 32 years old, I had found a passion I could truly call my own. It was in June of 2012 that I made the decision to step away from Commercial Real Estate after a year in the business and fully commit my time, energy and drive into my newly minted company: EntrepreneurOnFire LLC.

First things first: I knew I had to find a mentor. I was lucky: I had to look no further than 45 minutes up the road where Coach and Host of the popular podcast, Eventual Millionaire, Jaime Tardy, resided. I reached out to her via email and laid out exactly what I envisioned. I had no idea what her response would be, and when I saw her reply in my inbox, I held my breath and clicked open.

Much to my delight (and relief), the contents of her email stated that she thought my vision was an attainable, albeit demanding, goal. She agreed to mentor me during the critical "platform building" stage, and she let me know focus #1 was to attend Blogworld in NYC so I could rub elbows with those who would surely be my initial interviewees.

So, it was off to NYC in June of 2012 for my first ever conference, and I have to say, Blogworld was a massive success. I walked away with a verbal "yes" from several Entrepreneurs who turned out to be my initial interviewees. Cliff Ravenscraft, Adam Baker, David Risley, and others encouraged me to drive on with my dream, (although I'm sure they thought an episode a day was a little much for a noobie to handle).

I retuned to my condo in Maine invigorated, and I immediately got to work putting the pieces together for my launch, which was to come in just three short months. My "**Summer of Fire**" was intense. I out in very long hours and learned A LOT, and much credit needs to go to my mentor Jaime Tardy who guided me every step along the way.

## This concludes the preface to *Podcast Launch.*

From this point forward, I will walk you through exactly what I did to take EntrepreneurOnFire from an idea to a red-hot podcast that is currently being downloaded at a clip of over 950,000 times a month and generating six-figures in monthly income.

# Chapter 1: Identifying your podcast

Ready to start the process of creating a killer podcast? Let's dive in!

Note to reader: There are multiple video tutorials associated with this book. Go to __PodcastLaunchVideos.com__ to access each and every one!

## Step 1: Choose a topic/industry/niche that you are going to focus your podcast on.

With EntrepreneurOnFire, I knew who my target demographic was. I was creating a podcast for people like myself who were driving to work every day looking for Entrepreneurial content to consume. Also, the active types who were at the gym 5-days a week with headphones on, not listening to top 40 jams, but inspiring and motivating content.

I knew that EntrepreneurOnFire was going to resonate with this segment of the population. I was creating a show that would be sharing the journey of an incredible Entrepreneur every day of the week. With over 950,000 unique downloads a month, I have definitely found my audience. Let me help you find yours.

### Task #1: What niche are you trying to fill with your podcast?

The more specific you can be here the better.

### Task #2: Who is your avatar (i.e. your perfect listener)?

Be specific, and write down what type of person will become an avid listener of your podcast. Then, focus on creating the best podcast possible from their perspective. For an incredible post on this this topic, click or tap here.

99% of people fall well short here. Your avatar needs to be 1 single person. When you create this 1 person, every fork you come to in the road (and there will be thousands) will be a simple decision if you REALLY know your avatar. To check out my avatar, click or tap here and scroll down to the 2nd video.

# Step 2: Audio or video?

For me, this was a no-brainer once I had nailed down my avatar. My avatar would not be able to watch video while driving, running, or walking their dog. Audio was the obvious choice. However, video does have some legitimate pros for certain demographics and industries.

### Task #1: Weigh both options and proceed forward with what your avatar would want!

# Step 3: Self-host or co-host?

For EntrepreneurOnFire, it's not likely that I would have been able to find someone crazy enough to produce 30 podcasts a month, so this was an easy decision for me. However, there are some VERY successful podcasts (Internet Business Mastery, Tropical MBA) that are co-hosted and bring on guests quite often to make it a total of three people on the mic simultaneously.

**Task #1: Weigh both options and proceed forward with what your avatar would want!**

# Step 4: Interview format or Topic based?

With EntrepreneurOnFire, my vision was to share the journey of incredible Entrepreneurs with the world. That made my decision of an interview format quite easy.

Tim Paige and I teamed up and launched <u>Love Your Leap</u>, which is a show that we co-host, and chat about relevant struggles and obstacles that Entrepreneurs face. We do not bring on any guests, and just chat with each other. It's a lot of fun and very different from EntrepreneurOnFire's interview style.

**Task #1: Weigh both options and make a decision about what resonates best with you, the host, and what you think will resonate best with your listener.**

Below is a quick breakdown of what my task list looks like:

<u>**EntrepreneurOnFire**</u>

1) **Niche:** A business podcast that interviews today's most successful and inspiring Entrepreneurs 5-days a week. My avatar is someone who is looking to fill their commute, workout, or any other time with inspiring content that will encourage them to make their Entrepreneurial leap.

2) **Audio:** My avatar will listen while they are occupied with other activities.

3) **Self-host:** Who is crazy enough to do a show 5 days a week with me?

4) **Interview:** My vision is to share the journey of incredible Entrepreneurs via interviews.

## Mission Statement

Now it's time to write your mission statement. This is your true vision for your podcast.

## EntrepreneurOnFire's Mission Statement

To produce a daily podcast interviewing the worlds most inspiring and successful Entrepreneurs, sharing their journey and empowering listeners to make their Entrepreneurial leap.

CONGRATULATIONS! Now you know the niche you are filling, whom you are speaking to, and you have your mission statement to keep you on track. Now let's get down to the nitty gritty.

# Chapter 2: Equipment

The great opportunity with podcasting is being able to share your message with the world for an incredibly low cost. Let's go over the equipment you absolutely need, and the equipment that is optional.

Necessary:

- Computer
- Microphone
- Recording software

Optional:

- Mixer

Yep, you are reading correctly. This is all you need for equipment! I am going to go through these three components and share some different price points. I will also give you my opinion on where you should start off.

## Microphone

*Free option*: Built-in microphone. 99.9% of computers have a built-in microphone these days.

You can definitely produce a podcast going this route by just pressing the red button in your recording software and talking at your computer. I do not recommend this option since the audio quality will be lower than podcast listeners are used to hearing, and this will definitely detract from the number of repeat listeners you have.

That said, using a built-in microphone is a great option if you want to try recording a few episodes – just to make sure podcasting is something you want to pursue at a higher level.

*Low cost option*: Logitech ClearChat USB Headset, $29.99. This headset will plug right into your computer's USB port and will provide you with a decent quality, hands-free microphone. This is a great way to start, and once you get the hang of things, it will be an easy upgrade to the next option.

*Medium cost option*: ATR-2100, $59.99. This is my #1 recommendation by a long shot. When you combine cost and quality, nothing compares. If you can afford the $60 price tag…this is a MUST. This microphone also plugs into your USB port, and it is not a headset.

*High cost option*: Heil PR-40 (XLR connection, option for USB), $327.00. This is what I use, and you simply cannot beat the audio quality this microphone provides. It is important to note you will have to buy a separate cord if you want to plug the Heil directly into your USB. If you stick with the XLR, you will have to take the additional step and purchase a mixer.

I regularly update my "Recommended Podcast Equipment" here:

# Recording software

This software allows your voice to be recorded, edited, and converted into an MP3.

*Free options:*

For Mac: GarageBand. GarageBand is a software application for OS X and iOS that allows users to create music or podcasts.

For PC and Mac: Audacity. Audacity is an audio editor for recording, slicing, and mixing audio.

*Cost option:*

For both Mac and PC: Adobe Audition. This is what I use to record and edit every episode of EntrepreneurOnFire. You can purchase access on a monthly basis for $20 through the Adobe creative cloud. I HIGHLY recommend going this route if it's in your budget. In **Podcasters' Paradise**, we have over 40 video tutorials, which will turn you into an Adobe Audition PRO!

## Skype

In addition to the recording software option you choose, I recommend using Skype to place your interview calls. When you are recording your interviews via Skype (audio or video), below are your two best options (both are a one time cost of around $29):

For Mac: ECamm Call recorder: Automatically record and save call audio and video on your Mac.

For PC: Pamela: Automatically record and save call audio and video on your Mac.

In **Podcasters' Paradise,** we have video tutorials walking you through every step of this process!

*I record from Skype directly into Adobe Audition using my PreSonus Firestudio mixer.*

## Mixer *(optional)*

A mixer is an electronic device for combining, routing, and changing the level, timbre and/or dynamics of audio signals. Again, this piece of equipment is optional, but critical if you want to produce a high quality podcast. If you are going to go with a Heil PR-40 microphone and the XLR connection, a mixer is needed.

I use the Presonus Firestudio Project, $399.95. This mixer is an all-in-one, and in my mind, the best feature is that it allows me to record my audio and my interviewees' audio on separate tracks. There are a TON of benefits to this, such as silencing out background noise and cutting out parts of the audio if you talk over each other.

Well, there you have it! I hope you are way less intimidated now that you know how cost-effective and how few pieces of equipment you actually need to launch a podcast.

# Chapter 3: Recording and editing your audio

Video #1, 2, 3, 4, 5 associated with this chapter:

PodcastLaunchVideos.com

## Recording

Now that you understand what is needed for equipment, you're ready to press that little red button and start recording. I have created three videos that take you through the process of recording, editing, and exporting you audio as a MP3. Video #1 is for Audacity (PC and Mac), #2 is for GarageBand (Mac), and #3 is for Adobe Audition (PC and Mac – my favorite). Videos #4 and #5 show you how to record an interview over Skype using both Adobe Audition (#4) and eCamm Call Recorder (#5).

Go to PodcastLaunchVideos.com for tutorials on how to:

1. Record your audio

2. Edit your audio

3. Export as a MP3, which is the format you will want it in when you submit it to iTunes, Stitcher Radio, and Blackberry

4. Record an interview over Skype using both Adobe Audition and eCamm Call Recorder.

# Chapter 4: Intros and Outros

**Video #6 associated with this chapter <u>PodcastLaunchVideos.com</u>**

Your intros and outros are a time to give your listeners some key calls-to-action. With your first three episodes, you should use this time to:

1. Fully explain your podcast.

2. What you will be bringing to the table each episode.

3. What consistency you will be providing.

Setting your listeners' expectations is incredibly important. I cannot stress this point enough. EntrepreneurOnFire is successful because every day my listeners know there is a fresh episode waiting for them.

In your initial episodes, it is very important to let your audience know your production schedule. If you say you are going to release an episode every Wednesday, or every other Friday, that is great, but make sure you STICK TO YOUR SCHEDULE!

After your initial release, you can start inserting powerful calls-to-action in the intros and outros. At EntrepreneurOnFire, I change it up all the time. When I first launched, I asked my audience for an iTunes rating and review if they enjoyed the episode. Then, I asked for listeners to come to EntrepreneurOnFire.com and join my email list.

Now, I have a rotating schedule of seven intros and outros where I remind listeners of different products or services I have created and where they can find them.

To conclude, remember that as the Host, you have earned the right to use your intro and outro to promote yourself and your business. You are providing great content to your listeners for free, and a respectable call to action at the top and bottom of your episode will be received cordially.

I have found that at 60 seconds, you should be diving into your main content. You can go a little longer with the outro since people who are sticking around after you have concluded the main part of the episode obviously still have some interest in what you have to say.

One final piece of advice: don't make the mistake of recording a long, rambling intro. People have an incredible amount of choices these days, and if you cannot convince them quickly that the choice they've made to listen to the content you're providing is worthwhile, then they will click the back button and be out of your life forever.

## Resources you can use to create an intro and outro

TimThePaige.com: Tim is my #1 recommendation for your intro and outro. He is a 1-stop shop for an incredibly affordable price. Ask for the 'Fire' special and you'll be shocked at what you get for the cost!

MusicBakery.com: This is a great place to purchase royalty free music to add to your intro and outro.

Pond5.com: Similar to MusicBakery.com.

AudioJungle.com: Similar to MusicBakery.com.

**Make sure you spend the money to obtain royalty free music. This will ensure you avoid legal entanglements down the road.

FIVERR.com: This site allows you to find a voice artist you like and submit a job to them for just $5. You get what you pay for, and your intro/outro will be a lot lower quality than Tim will provide you, (with more work involved on your side too) but I have found some diamonds in the rough.

In video #6, I show you how to add an intro and outro to your audio recording in Adobe Audition.

Go to **PodcastLaunchVideos.com** for access to every video tutorial.

# Chapter 5: Tagging, uploading, and embedding your MP3

**Video #7, 8, 9 associated with this chapter**

PodcastLaunchVideos.com

Now you know how to record your audio, edit to your fancy, and export as a MP3. Now it's time to:

1. "Tag" the MP3 file

2. Upload to your Media Host

3. Schedule the release to the major directories: iTunes, Stitcher, and Blackberry

## Tagging

This is the process of adding your artwork (1400x1400 min, 2048x2048 max), show title, description, and copyright information into the MP3 before you upload. This will ensure:

1. Your artwork shows up in the iTunes, Stitcher Radio, and Blackberry store.

2. Your title and description are viewable when a person subscribes.

I have created a video (#7) that takes you through a step-by-step process of:

1. Opening up your MP3 using the free software program ID3 Editor.

2. Tagging all the necessary information.

3. Updating this information onto the MP3.

Go to PodcastLaunchVideos.com for access to every video tutorial.

It is important to note that at the time of this publication, iTunes was "highly recommending" that your podcast's artwork come in the format of 1400x1400. If you do not have a designer, Fivvr.com is a great place to get designs for just $5. You get what you pay for here, but there are a lot of talented people on this network who provide a great value.

If you really want to step it up, 99Designs is a GREAT place to get killer artwork.

## Media Host

Securing a Media Host is a necessary expense for producing a podcast. If you try and store your MP3's on your website and your podcast becomes popular, your site's speed will suffer dramatically. This is because listeners will eat up all your bandwidth while streaming the episode straight from your site. Amazon S3 allows you to store your media files for a very low cost and charges you by the bandwidth you use.

My recommended Media Host – and the one I use for my multiple podcasts – is Liberated Syndication, or LibSyn.com offer code "FIRE". They are a Media Host dedicated to podcasters and provide an incredible format that will host your media, publish your podcast, and allow you to utilize their unlimited bandwidth all for one set monthly cost. (Plans run between $5 and $75 depending on your usage.)

**EntrepreneurOnFire is one of nine affiliates of Libsyn. If you would like to receive the remainder of the first month and the following month for free, simply enter the code "**FIRE**" while setting up your account.**

I have created another video (#8) that takes you through the following, step-by-step:

1. Setting up a LibSyn account.
2. Adding artwork, a show description, categories, and other necessary details to your account.
3. Uploading your media to LibSyn.
4. Adding your title and description.
5. Publishing your podcast.
6. Scheduling time-specific releases of your podcast.

Don't forget the code "**FIRE**" will get you up to 2 free months!

Go to <u>PodcastLaunchVideos.com</u> for access to every video tutorial.

If you have a website, you will want to stream your podcast on your site. Many visitors will appreciate the opportunity to listen to it while they browse. I have created a video tutorial (#9) that takes you through the following, step-by-step:

1. How to download and install the Wordpress plugin in PowerPress.

2. How to find and copy the Direct Download URL from LibSyn.com.

3. How to paste that URL into you're the powerpress plugin to allow your podcast to be streamed or downloaded from the post of your choice.

Go to <u>PodcastLaunchVideos.com</u> for access to every video tutorial.

# Chapter 6: Submitting your Podcast to iTunes, Stitcher Radio, and Blackberry

**Video #10 associated with this chapter**

PodcastLaunchVideos.com

Let's step back for a moment. Now that you have the skills necessary to record, edit, export, tag, upload, schedule, and post; what's next? It's finally time to submit your podcast to the three major directories: iTunes, Stitcher Radio, and Blackberry!

I have created a video (#10) that walks you through the entire process. It shows you how to:

1. Access your RSS feed from LibSyn.

2. Submit this feed to iTunes, Stitcher Radio, and Blackberry.

3. Sit back, and wait for your podcast to be accessible to the world.

   **Once you have submitted your feed and it has been accepted, iTunes, Stitcher Radio, and Blackberry will automatically update every time you publish/release a podcast from LibSyn.

Go to PodcastLaunchVideos.com for access to every video tutorial.

# Chapter 7: Launching your Podcast right

**Video #11 associated with this chapter PodcastLaunchVideos.com**

This chapter is going to be focused on launching your podcast the right way instead of the way 99% of podcasters launch. iTunes is a destination that millions of listeners are going to every day in search of content. For podcasters, this is a goldmine because every day people are learning about the on demand, targeted, passionate, and free content podcasts provide, and they begin their search for ones that best fit their passions.

## New and Noteworthy

The absolute BEST real estate in the entire podcast universe is the New and Noteworthy section in the iTunes Podcast Store. The first two rows that you see are the top 100 "New and Noteworthy" podcasts.

To be featured in the New and Noteworthy section you need to:

1. Have a podcast that has been released within the last 8 weeks.

2. Have a large enough subscriber base.

3. Have a substantial amount of downloads.

4. Have a growing number of 5-star ratings and reviews.

I have published multiple podcasts on the iTunes platform, and I can tell you from first-hand experience that it does not take many subscribers, downloads, or 5-star reviews to get you into the New and Noteworthy section. There are simply not many podcasts that fit the noteworthy requirement. In this chapter, I'm going to make sure your podcast does.

I really want to stress the point that you have a mere 8 weeks to be featured within the best podcast advertising real estate on the planet. You NEED to make sure you are taking full advantage of every single one of these 56 glorious days.

EntrepreneurOnFire was ranked as the #1 Business Podcast in iTunes New and Noteworthy for all 8 weeks, and the organic traffic I received as a result of this was HUGE! This placement has a phenomenal snowball effect: once you appear in the New and Noteworthy, listeners who show up to search for content see you right away. They check you out; subscribe to your podcast; drive up your download numbers, which in turn drives up your ranking in iTunes; and soon enough you're being found more often and easily!

So, the question here is: how can you maximize this amazing opportunity? Below, I list out the KEY actions you must take prior to – and during – your launch, why they are so important, and why they will be so effective.

# Pre-Launch

Make sure you are doing these activates BEFORE you launch:

## 1. Build your platform

Once you launch and people start to enjoy the content of your show, they are going to want a headquarters where they can learn more. You need a system that allows your listeners to share their wants, needs, desires, and most importantly, their email addresses.

## 2. Create a Website

You need to start with a Website that will be your home base and that adds value for your listeners. This is where everything will spring from, and it is yours alone to have and control.

If you go to EntrepreneurOnFire.com, then you will find a fully functioning site where I post and stream every episode, including a Show Notes page that sums up each show. This drives traffic back to my website, where I can then offer my listeners a lot of great value.

I also have a resources page, which includes affiliate links, coaching sessions, and other valuable resources that, in addition to helping listeners, helps EntrepreneurOnFire earn money. I will delve more into this in a future chapter.

Ready to create your website? We have an amazing a free

tutorial for you that will walk you through the process of acquiring a free domain an setting up your Wordpress site through our recommended web host, BlueHost. You can find the free tutorial here!

## 3. Start an email list

One of your top priorities with producing a podcast and growing an audience is to simultaneously be growing an email list. There is no better way to connect with your fans and listeners than through their inbox, and as you can see, at EntrepreneurOnFire, it is a priority on my site: front and center is "Join and receive our eBook!"

I have grown my email list to over 20,000 subscribers this way, and it is one of my most valuable commodities!

>> Click or tap here << to get Aweber, my #1 recommended affordable email marketing provider. Watch my free tutorial here!

## 4. Get LeadPages!

There is really nothing more to say here. LeadPages will be integral in every part of your business, and is worth EVERY penny.

>> Click or tap here << to get LeadPages. Watch my free

tutorial here!

## 5. Be Social!

Your listeners all have their favorite Social Media sites, and you have to make sure they have a platform to share your show on each and every one of them. I have a Virtual Assistant (VA) who works 40 hours a week managing my Facebook, Twitter, LinkedIn, Pinterest, and Google + accounts. Now, I am not saying you need a VA when you first launch, but I DO want to illustrate how seriously I take Social Media, and the rewards of this attitude are evident to me daily.

At the time of this publication, EntrepreneurOnFire had over 14,000 Facebook fans, over 28,000 Twitter followers, and huge audiences on G+, Pinterest, and LinkedIn. I interact with listeners on each of these platforms daily, and I can say with confidence that Social Media has really helped get EntrepreneurOnFire's name out to as large an audience as possible.

## 6. Create multiple episodes

Before you launch, have at least three shows completed, and publish all three at the SAME time. Almost every show launches with one measly episode. This is a huge mistake for a number of reasons:

- When people stumble across a podcast that only has one episode, they are going to wonder whether or not it is a serious show. Listeners have seen their fair share of "one and done" podcasts.

- If people see just one episode and decide to give it try, they will likely just "listen" and not **subscribe** since there is really nothing to subscribe to. This will diminish your chances of obtaining subscribers significantly.

- Let's say 100 people find your podcast in the first week. If you only have one episode available, you will have 100 downloads. If you have three episodes, people will likely subscribe **and** download all three episodes, as it's just one press of a button to do so. Presto: you have 300 downloads and a ton of subscribers. Your chances of popping into New and Noteworthy just skyrocketed, and as I explained earlier, once you are in New and Noteworthy, the magical snowball effect begins. Sit back, and let the downloads roll in!

Go to **PodcastLaunchVideos.com** for access to every video tutorial.

# Chapter 8: Building your audience

Video #12 associated with this chapter

PodcastLaunchVideos.com

You have taken all the right steps and your podcast is about to go live.

Now what?

Be prepared; hitting the submit button in iTunes does not translate to having your podcast appear immediately. iTunes, Stitcher Radio, and Blackberry all have a review process where they approve each podcast, and it can take anywhere from four to 72 hours depending on the day of the week you submit (and their current backlog).

EntrepreneurOnFire was accepted six hours after submission, whereas The Great Business Experiment: Kickstarter took closer to 72 hours. (Note that I submitted the latter on a Friday over the Christmas holiday.)

Before we progress further, take a second to pat yourself on the back – you did it! That was a lot of hard work you just put in. Let me be the first to say, "Congratulations!"

## Focus: Follow One Course Until Success

Your focus is to maximize the eight weeks of New and Noteworthy eligibility you have. Your podcast episodes are live. You need subscribers, downloads, ratings, and reviews. Here what's next:

## Platform

This is where your platform comes in, and YOU are your best advocate. Reach out to everyone: family, friends, people on Facebook, Twitter, past interviewees, upcoming interviewees, anyone with an iTunes account – simply ask them to take a minute to subscribe and give your show a 5-star rating and review. I have created a quick video (#12) that you are free to share. It will take your listeners through step-by-step process of how to submit a rating and review on iTunes.

Go to PodcastLaunchVideos.com for access to every video tutorial.

At this point, you've done more to set your show up for success than 99% of the other podcasters out there. Continue to focus, continue to produce incredible content, and continue to ask people to subscribe, rate, and review your show.

EntrepreneurOnFire has over 1600 5-star ratings, all given in less than 15-months. I started with zero, just like you. Every time someone emailed to thank me for the show, I thanked them for listening, and then asked for a rating as an extension of their thanks.

I also let every interviewee I have on the show know that a rating and review from them would hold a lot of weight. This method will gain you ratings and reviews at a steady pace. The average podcast has less than 10 reviews; you'll soon catapult them in this department, and subsequently, in the rankings as well!

Remember: you are providing great value and content for free, and most people welcome the opportunity to say thanks. You just have to provide them with this opportunity in a kind and friendly manner.

## Momentum

EntrepreneurOnFire currently generates in excess of 30,000 downloads EVERY day from people in over 145 countries, and that number continues to grow as more and more people discover and subscribe to the show. How did I build my audience from zero on September 20th 2012 to over 950,000 every month a mere 2+ years later? As always… I share all!

During the summer of 2012, I interviewed 40 Entrepreneurs in order to prepare for EntrepreneurOnFire's launch. I knew I was taking on a lot of pressure by pledging out of the gates to be the only podcast that interviewed one incredible Entrepreneur 7-days a week.

I also knew that in order to get my momentum going I needed to launch with a large buffer and keep that buffer steady. For someone producing a weekly podcast, eight podcasts in the can would be the equivalent to this, so no need to be scared by the number 40 if you do not plan on hosting a daily podcast.

I launched on September 22nd. Three podcasts went live on launch day, and one more episode went live every day thereafter according to my schedule.

Now that EntrepreneurOnFire was live, I began to implement all the techniques I outlined above. Every morning, my first activity was to reach out to that day's interviewee and let them know their interview was live, and that I would be honored if they would share this with their audience.

I made sure I had scheduled posts lined up for Facebook, Twitter, G+, and LinkedIn that would go out periodically throughout the day to catch people who would be interested in listening to that day's interview.

This tactic works. Every day, my guest shares their wonderful interview with their massive audience. My guest's audience jumps at the opportunity to listen to their beloved Entrepreneur, and many become subscribers after enjoying the fascinating journey each guest shares. Once they find out it's a daily podcast, they begin to look forward to each new episode.

This initial push got EntrepreneurOnFire in the New and Noteworthy section, and suddenly, hundreds of people were "discovering" EntrepreneurOnFire daily as they came to iTunes in search of inspiring and motivating content.

By the middle of October, EntrepreneurOnFire was averaging over

1,000 unique downloads a day; by November, that number was over 2,500. In December, it jumped to 3,500, and by mid-January, EntrepreneurOnFire was averaging over 5,000 unique downloads a day. As of this publication, EntrepreneurOnFire has reached 26,860 downloads in a single day! Still not convinced podcasting is catching on?

If you are producing a weekly or bi-weekly podcast, you should not compare your download numbers to these, as you will simply not have as many "downloads" possible with fewer episodes available. With that said, you should be seeing a similar trend of a growing audience if you are doing everything we have outlined.

In summation, you build an audience with content, consistency, and promotion, in that order. Content is king. No matter how consistent you are and how great your promoting is, without great content, nobody will share, and nobody will return.

Also, without consistency, listeners have a hard time trusting that you're going to continue to produce great content worthy of the time they are investing.

Finally: promotion. No one should be a bigger advocate of the podcast you are producing than you are. Fire Nation sees how much time and effort I spend promoting EntrepreneurOnFire, and they know I am standing behind my show and putting my reputation on the line every single day.

Go to **PodcastLaunchVideos.com** for access to every video tutorial.

# Chapter 9: Monetizing

*"You can have everything in life you want, if you will just help other people get what they want."* ~ Zig Ziglar

The most recurring question I am asked in interviews, in emails, after speeches and really just in general is, *"How do you make money?"*

This is a fair question. With the amount of time, effort and value most people devote to their Podcast, it only seems fair that you should be compensated financially. However, it's important to go about this in the right way and to really understand that you need to be seen as a person providing value first and foremost. **If you are successful in doing this, the money will follow.**

As past interviewee MJ DeMarco stated on EntrepreneurOnFire, *"If you want to make millions, you have to help millions."* I have adjusted that slightly for EntrepreneurOnFire to read, *"If you want to make millions, you have to inspire millions."*

I like the word inspire for EntrepreneurOnFire because my goal is to inspire and motivate my listeners to have the courage to pursue their dreams. What is your big, hairy, audacious goal?

This will be the 3rd time I mention it now, but as it's the number one question I am asked, I feel like people want to know as many details as possible.

In September of 2013, EntrepreneurOnFire began publishing our income reports to share all of our earnings, expenses, successes and failures. I recommend studying these to see which strategies appeal to you, and then go ahead and try to implement some in your own business!

Here are some details on each of the income streams we talk about:

## Affiliate Commission

EntrepreneurOnFire.com, the website, receives around 2,000 unique visits every day, all of which is traffic driven straight from the podcast. People arrive at EntrepreneurOnFire.com because they want to learn more about Fire Nation, and because they want to further their knowledge about Entrepreneurship. My Resources Page is one of the top three highest trafficked pages on my site and is a compilation of all the resources I recommend to Fire Nation as they start their own journey.

I have used every one of the resources I recommend, and I have affiliate relationships with each vendor. When a visitor clicks on a link from my Resources Page, a unique URL alerts the vendor that they came from my page. If a purchase is made, I receive a commission. In the 15 months following the launch of EntrepreneurOnFire, my Resources Page was responsible for over $50,000 in affiliates sales. This is not necessarily "retire early" money, but nothing to shy away from, either.

On that note, there are several techniques you can use to drive even more affiliate traffic through your affiliate links, like what I did with my BlueHost link specifically: I created a 7-minute video tutorial just for anyone who uses my affiliate link, and I promote this in one of my intros on EntrepreneurOnFire.

Lesson: add value to everything that you do!

## Partnerships

I have just recently partnered up with Audible.com. They reached out to me, and when they explained their program I realized it made a lot of sense and aligned very well with EntrepreneurOnFire.

They provided me with a unique link, and every time someone uses this link to subscribe for a free 30-day trial, they will receive a free audio book, and I will receive a little commission check. I love the fact my audience gets something of great value for free, and because I know, like and trust Audible, it makes the relationship a win/win/win (my audience wins, I win and Audible wins!).

AudibleTrial.com/Fire is the special URL they provided me with, so if you feel like grabbing an audio book for free, check it out! I recommend **The One Thing** by Gary Keller.

## Coaching

As I've mentioned before, one of the great benefits of being a Podcaster is that you are in the ears of your listeners. A majority of my audience consumes EntrepreneurOnFire on their way to work, while at the gym, or while taking their dog for a walk. This gives me a captive and engaged audience who hears my voice day after day, episode after episode. If the content you provide is great, then your listeners will begin to know, like and trust you.

When Entrepreneurs are ready to take their own leap, they often look for coaches/mentors to guide them through the unknown terrain they are about to face. When you host a show, you gain instant credibility and authority in that niche, and you have the opportunity to develop an intimate connection with your audience by providing them with the content they're looking for.

When it comes time for your audience to reach out to someone for guidance, you are a perfect candidate. Because you are an expert in your particular field, you will be able to impart priceless knowledge and experience upon your students, and earn a great income while doing so.

When I began the journey of creating EntrepreneurOnFire, I reached out to a mentor in my field, Jaime Tardy of The Eventual Millionaire. I paid her $1,000 a month for three months to be my coach. That investment proved to be invaluable, as the advice she gave me, the connections she was responsible for making, and the technical advice she shared allowed me to save an incredible amount of time, heartache, and money in the long run.

At EntrepreneurOnFire, I offer a mentorship program and have made the decision to keep my number of students to a minimum. However, depending on what your own goals are in becoming a mentor, you can develop as large a coaching program as you want, whether it be in a one-on-one format, a small group, or even a large mastermind.

## Masterminds

With the mentality that I want to impact Entrepreneurs on a personal level, I launched an Elite Mastermind Tribe called FireNationElite. We are currently a closed mastermind, as we decided to cap our Tribe at 100 members. However, you can always find out more and join the wait list here: FireNationElite.

FireNationElite (FireNationElite.com) is a great example of how I've created a Mastermind that generates recurring revenue, as each member pays quarterly to be a part of the Mastermind. EntrepreneurOnFire generates $13,500 every month from this venture, and again, this would not be possible if it weren't for the credibility I've gained in my niche via the podcast.

## Sponsorships

At the time of this publication, sponsorships made up about 20% of

EntrepreneurOnFire's monthly income, and in Januray 2015 alone we generated over $60k in sponsorship revenue!

How did we get started with sponsors? Great question. I'm going to do an insanely deep dive into the world of Podcast sponsorships right here, right now.

## How we got started with Sponsors: A Brief Overview

In March 2013 – around the six-month mark of the business – my download numbers and rankings in iTunes, (which were both a direct result of providing amazing content and value to my listeners for free), began to attract sponsors.

Once sponsors started reaching out to me, I knew I had to figure out what my number was going to be – my number meaning, at what cost would I bring sponsors on the show and dilute my content?

Once I figured out my number (I'll dive into all of this in more detail in a bit), my number one priority was to first make sure that every sponsor I brought on the show was relevant and helpful to my audience. If a sponsor approached me with a product or service that I knew wouldn't prove to be beneficial to my audience, then it was (and still is) very easy for me to say, "No."

During the month of April 2013 – our first month with sponsors – we had our first 5-figure month ($12,584) at EntrepreneurOnFire, with 85% of our revenue generated coming straight from sponsorships. It was then that we realized sponsorships could provide a lot of valuable resources to our audience, while also bringing in a very steady, healthy income.

It all sounds so easy, right?

**Let's get real: Can you start a podcast today and have sponsors lined up at your doorstep tomorrow?**

No.

Can you start a podcast today focused on a niche you're passionate and knowledgeable about (the knowledge can come), work hard for a significant amount of time (6 months... a year?), build a captive and engaged audience, and THEN have sponsors beating down your door to get in front of your listeners?

Yes!

**Let's take a minute to turn back the clock and go through my first six months, which we'll call the "Pre-Sponsorship Days", so you can get an idea of *why* sponsors started to approach me in the first place.**

I launched on September 22nd, 2012 to four straight days of crickets... AKA no downloads. Zero, zip, zilch (unless you count my own personal downloads :-). Then, as my guests began sharing their interviews with their massive audiences, the download numbers began to climb.

Next thing I knew, I was ranking high in the New and Noteworthy section of iTunes, which began to drive a ton of organic traffic my way.

How did I get my guests to share their interview with their massive audiences? **I just asked them.**

My first email every morning was (and still is) to my featured guest, whose interview is going live on that particular day. Here's what the email said back then (I've tweaked this a bit since, but the main message remains):

> *<Guest's first name>,*
>
> *Thank you so much for sharing your amazing journey on EntrepreneurOnFire. I would be honored if you would share with your audience. Here are the links if you decide to do so. <insert links here>*
>
> *Thank you again for Igniting the world!*

Is this email corny? Maybe.

Is it effective? Heck Yeah! :-)

Soon, the combination of EntrepreneurOnFire being shared with others' massive audiences daily, and the organic traffic coming my way as a result of ranking high in New and Noteworthy, got the EntrepreneurOnFire snowball effect rolling.

Our guests sharing EntrepreneurOnFire with their audiences resulted in more downloads; more downloads resulted in higher rankings in New and Noteworthy; higher rankings in New and Noteworthy resulted in more organic downloads; and more coal was being added to the fire daily!

Within two and a half months after our launch, EntrepreneurOnFire was generating over 100,000 unique downloads every single month.

This success landed me an offer to be a speaker at NMX Blogworld in Vegas, January 2013. This was the same conference I had attended just six months prior, like a baby fawn with eyes wide open to the crazy world of online Entrepreneurs that just days before I knew nothing about.

The conference was powerful, and the credibility from speaking at NMX in Vegas landed EntrepreneurOnFire interviews with Tim Ferriss and Barbara Corcoran in rapid succession.

## Then, at month six, things really started to take off: A deep dive into how sponsorships work

In mid-March, I was approached by three sponsors. I kindly replied by asking for a week to consider the opportunity, and then I immediately got on the phone with a friend and fellow Podcaster who had been in this game for a while to ask for some unbiased advice.

During our conversation, I found out what sponsors have come to expect from sponsorships and Podcast hosts.

**I'm about to reveal what I learned on that call, and in the eight months that have followed while working with over 15 sponsors for EntrepreneurOnFire.**

Below is the "Industry Standard". Always remember that YOU are the host of your show and that you should propose any arrangement you feel is best for you and your listeners. If the interested sponsor is not game, then bye, bye.

I only partner with sponsors who will add value to Fire Nation, and I never hesitate to turn away sponsors that do not have my listeners' best interests at heart.

I have created many valuable relationships this way, and many of my current sponsors stay with EntrepreneurOnFire month after month because I strive to create a win/win in every partnership. I will share how and why in just a minute...

# Industry Standard

The current "Industry Standard" Podcast sponsorship is a combo 15-second Pre-Roll and a 60-second Mid-Roll.

## Pre-Roll

Prior to launching into the main content, the host will talk about the sponsor's product or service for 15-seconds. On EntrepreneurOnFire, our Pre-Rolls are right after the intro music. Click or tap here to listen to a sample.

## Mid-Roll

There is a lot more flexibility here. The Mid-Roll is typically inserted somewhere in the 40 - 70% mark of the Podcast episode. The host will talk about the sponsor's product or service for 60-seconds this time, often sharing a personal story if possible.

On EntrepreneurOnFire, our Mid-Rolls are right before "The Lightning Round", which puts them close to the 70% mark on most episodes. Click or tap here to listen to a sample.

**Another opportunity for sponsorships is during the outro. EntrepreneurOnFire has experimented with this for the first time in Q4 2013 with great results. This is the last call to action your listeners will hear, and on EntrepreneurOnFire, it's proving to be a call to action that is driving results.

## So what exactly are these "Industry Standards" in terms of pricing?

- A 15-second Pre-Roll commands $18 per 1000 CPMs (listens)

- A 60-second Mid-Roll commands $25 per 1000 CPMs

(listens)

For ease of math purposes, let's say your podcast averages 10,000 listens per episode:

- 18 x 10 (for the 10,000 listens) = $180 is the cost to the sponsor for a Pre-Roll

- 25 x 10 (for the 10,000 listens) = $250 is the cost to the sponsor for a Mid-Roll

**Therefore, your 10,000 listens per episode would cost a sponsor $430 for a Pre-Roll/Mid-Roll combo.**

Let's say you allow two sponsors per episode; now you are making $860 per episode.

- 4 episodes a month: $3,440

- 8 episodes a month: $6,880

- 30 episodes a month: $25,800 (now you can see one of the reasons why I love doing a daily show!)

The above model is only the "industry standard", and I have structured deals with both higher and lower CPMs; however, most of my deals are at this CPM rate.

So a common question after reading through this stuff is, *"How do I know what my 'average listens' are so I can determine my CPM rate?"*

Great question! Look at the download numbers of your episodes starting at six weeks out. Remember, you're guaranteeing a MINIMUM number of listens, so you need to be confident that you are fulfilling your end of the contract.

Once you see that EVERY episode is over a certain number of downloads by week six, that is your CPM. You can adjust this as often as monthly, (although I adjust quarterly, as it build a strong rapport with my sponsors to know that I'm willing to make this as beneficial for them as possible.) And yes, this does mean that if I guarantee 16,000 listens per episodes, and one of my episodes ends up getting 19,000 listens within the six weeks, that I am in fact "giving away" 3,000 listens to my sponsor for free.

To be clear, sponsors only care about how many downloads you are guaranteeing for the specific episode they are sponsoring. Go to your stats, look at the downloads you have PER EPISODE, and use that information to find your CPM rate.

## Pricing Model: CPM vs CPA

There are three routes you can take with your sponsors:

- Cost per mille (CPM): Cost per thousand views (listens in the Podcast world)

- Cost per Acquisition (CPA): Cost to acquire one customer

- You name the price, sponsors say yes or no. (This model is underrated for newer shows, and I like it... Remember, this is YOUR show!) This gives you the opportunity to reach out to newer companies who, like you are just trying to make a name for their business. If your message and goals align, then you might find a sponsorship fit sooner than you expected.

## Cost per mille (CPM)

This is the only way I deal with sponsors. If a sponsor wants to partner with EntrepreneurOnFire, then I will send them a proposal, and they can accept, reject, or negotiate.

Sponsors who try and negotiate with EntrepreneurOnFire have not had a ton of luck, as we receive way more inquiries (demand) then we could ever accept (supply).

My Q4 2013 sponsorship inventory was 100% sold out by September 2013 because my current sponsors all accepted my proposal when I sent it, which was based off the current industry standards. Those who tried to negotiate missed out on reaching EntrepreneurOnFire's massive audience.

## Cost per Acquisition (CPA)

One of the first ways I started monetizing with EntrepreneurOnFire was by using this model.

In Podcasters' Paradise I have a great video tutorial that walks you through the entire process of setting up a partnership with Audible, where you will get paid $15 for every person you send to their sales page that results in a sign up for a free audio book and free 30-day membership.

There were a couple months in a row where I generated between $2-3k per month using this model, and I was making Audible very happy. For those of you that have heard me say "EOFireBook.com", that was its original use.

## So why not bring more sponsors on?

Valid question! I will say once again: Your podcast is your show, and therefore it's your decision. However, my opinion on this matter is as follows:

I am a believer in the law of diminishing returns. In this case, I believe having three or more Pre-Roll and Mid-Roll sponsors is bad for everyone involved.

**It's bad for the sponsor.** Their message gets diminished, less listener action is being taken, and therefore, it's less likely that the sponsor will stay with you when it comes time to talk about extending your agreement.

**It's bad for the listener.** Your listener loves listening to Podcasts because it's free, it's on demand, and they don't have to put up with annoying commercials like they do with the radio. Podcast sponsorships work so well because it is YOU, the host, that is promoting the product or service, and your listeners trust you.

That trust will deteriorate if you make it seem more about the sponsorships than the listener. My listeners understand that after 30 seconds of me sharing two 15-second sponsorship slots, we will dive into the content. 30-seconds is not too much to ask, especially when my sponsors are all relevant to Entrepreneurs.

**Finally, it's bad for the host... you!** Why? Your goal is to provide so much value and high-quality content that your listeners not only keep coming back for more, but they tell their friends and family about you. Your goal is to provide great content, increase your listener base, and by default, increase the amount each sponsor pays you per sponsorship.

The math is simple. It's better to have two sponsors paying you $430 per episode than three paying you $287 for all the reasons above (and every other obvious one).

I will never have more than two Pre-Rolls and two Mid-Rolls on EntrepreneurOnFire because I care about Fire Nation.

Also, as previously stated, I will only partner with sponsors that I believe will benefit Fire Nation in their Entrepreneurial journey.

Don't believe me? Quick story:

I was approached by a Pay-Day Loan company that offered me double my going rate to sponsor EntrepreneurOnFire. I do not believe in Pay-Day loans for many reasons - especially as a recommendation for Fire Nation - so my answer was simple: No.

Saying yes would have generated $18k MORE in sponsorship revenue for Q4. Not even close to worth it... no dollar amount would be.

Show the same care for your audience, and you will be better serving yourself, your sponsor, and most importantly, your listener.

## When should I bring on sponsors?

My first recommendation to each Podcaster that is interested in going the sponsorship route is to sit down and think about the LEAST amount of money it would take for you to dilute your podcast with a sponsorship.

Did I just say dilute? Yep... and I meant it.

Dilute is not meant as a dirty word here. It is meant as a reality. When you bring on a sponsor, no matter how relevant, and no matter how awesome, you are on some level diluting the message of your podcast.

You're going to turn off some listeners, (although very few if you do it right); you're going to be sending some listeners away on actions that do not involve your platform; and finally, you will be distracting some focus from the main content of your Podcast.

Are any of these things bad? Not necessarily. But I bring them up because they should come with a minimum price tag. Sit down and come up with that baseline price tag: what's your number?

Your listeners are valuable, don't sell them out as otherwise.

For me, $500 was my baseline number. I said to myself that if EntrepreneurOnFire could bring in $500 per episode, that would be $15k per month at 100% capacity, and for me, that made sense. Anything less - nope, not ready yet.

In April, I hit that magic number, and my sponsorship revenue has been growing ever since!

**What is your number?**

If you know your number, you will be in a MUCH better position come negotiation time with your sponsors.

## How do I find sponsors?

You want to start by really drilling down and knowing exactly what your niche is.

Then, ask yourself, "What companies currently market to my niche?" Is your Podcast about raising children? I am sure Babies 'R Us would love to offer value to your audience. Fishing? L.L. Bean and Cabelas are already lining up!

Another option: listen to Podcasts within your niche. Do they have sponsors? If so, a well-crafted email to that same sponsor could yield a partnership. It has for me on numerous occasions.

## How should I approach sponsors?

Well that's easy: just email them! Once you find a sponsor that you're interested in doing business with, email them and let them know how it would benefit them to sponsor your show (very important, I repeat: let them know how it would benefit them to sponsor your show.)

Some things you'll want to include in the email are:

- A description of your audience (to prove that your listeners would be interested in the product or service your sponsor offers)

- Some stats to back up any claims you're making (percentage of listeners who match their audience, or # of listens your Podcast episodes average, or even things like "I've been featured in the New & Noteworthy and What's Hot sections of iTunes, and have been featured as a Top Podcast in Stitcher")

- An actual proposal (a separate attachment) that details your "request" or "offer" to them. Include details like the number of slots you'd like them to buy, the cost per slot, and how long you'd like them to sponsor for (could be one month, or it could be an entire year).

## I have interested sponsors, now what?

Congrats! Now all you have to do is let your sponsors know what your download numbers are and what it will cost for them to sponsor an episode. They can take it or leave it.

At some point, your download numbers may be able to be inserted into the above "Industry Standard" CPM rate and command a higher price than your minimum baseline number. At that point, it's time to go back to the negotiating table with your sponsor and start increasing the amount you receive per episode.

## Summation

Building an audience is an incredible way to create a viable business, and Podcasting is an incredible way to build an audience. That's obviously the model we chose to follow here at EntrepreneurOnFire.

Everything I've just shared about sponsorships and all of the other streams of income we have here are EntrepreneurOnFire is to help you turn your podcast or business into a viable one, and I hope you are able to take some of the information provided here to create your own freedom.

INCREDLE video tutorials, templates, and guides can be found in Podcasters' Paradise.

# Chapter 10: Conclusion

If you have followed the steps laid out in the previous chapters and in the video tutorials, then I have no doubt you have – or shortly will – release a great Podcast.

Podcasting is an incredible opportunity for anyone looking to venture out into a sparsely populated land that holds vast wealth and resources. You would be joining pioneers like me, who are staking our claim in this exciting new world and experiencing an incredible journey every day.

I hope you look at EntrepreneurOnFire.com as a resource that can help guide you on this journey. Please feel free to reach out to me with any questions you may have.

Oh, and lastly, **I would be a horrible coach** if I did not follow my own advice and end this book with one final call to action:

If you received value from the words and videos I have created for you here, please take a minute to leave a review in the Amazon store for my book, _Podcast Launch_. It would truly mean a lot to me. If you do submit a review, let me know. I have an incredible bonus video that I will share with you, Mr. or Mrs. leaver-of-reviews.

Simply email me and share that you left a review in Amazon (even if you did not buy the book from Amazon you can still leave a review) and I will respond with the password to unlock the bonus video! (no proof necessary…I trust you)

Finally, are you ready to CREATE ~ GROW ~ & MONETIZE your Podcast? Then join Podcasters' Paradise, the #1 Podcasting community with 200+ video tutorials, a private Facebook community with over 2000 other Podcasters, and monthly webinars with todays top Podcasters!

Best of luck in your Podcasting journey, and **Prepare to Ignite**!

~ John Lee Dumas

John@EntrepreneurOnFire.com

FreePodcastCourse.com

TheWebinarCourse.com

EOFire.com

Made in the USA
Lexington, KY
27 January 2018